A Troll First-Start® Tall Tale

Johnny Appleseed

GOES a'PLANTING

by Patsy Jensen • illustrated by Pat Hoggan

Troll Associates

John Chapman is one American folk hero who was a real person. He earned the nickname of Johnny Appleseed through his work planting apple orchards all over the country long ago.

A tall tale is an unusual story that has been exaggerated as it is retold over the years. Some of the things Johnny is said to have done probably never happened. But what is true about his story is his unique kindness to people and animals, and his love of the American wilderness.

Library of Congress Cataloging-in-Publication Data

Jensen, Patricia.
    Johnny Appleseed goes a'planting / by Patricia A. Jensen;
illustrated by Patricia M. Hoggan.
        p.   cm.— (A Troll first-start tall tale)
    ISBN 0-8167-3159-4 (lib. bdg.)   ISBN 0-8167-3160-8 (pbk.)
    1. Appleseed, Johnny, 1774-1845—Juvenile literature.   2. Apple
growers—United States—Biography—Juvenile literature.   3. Frontier
and pioneer life—Middle West—Juvenile literature.   [1. Appleseed,
Johnny, 1774-1845.   2. Apple growers.   3. Frontier and pioneer
life.]   I. Hoggan, Pat, ill.   II. Title.   III. Series.
SB63.C46J46   1994
634'.11'092—dc20
[B]   93-4811

Johnny Appleseed's real name was John Chapman. He got his nickname because he planted apple seeds everywhere he went.

Johnny was born on September 26, 1774 in Massachusetts. His father was a farmer. Johnny liked to help with farm chores.

Johnny's favorite chore was to take care of the apple orchard. He loved to climb apple trees and pick the shiny, red fruit.

When Johnny was a young man, people began to move west to settle in Ohio and other faraway places. These pioneers had to clear land, build their own houses, and plant crops. They did not have time to plant apple trees.

Johnny was sorry to hear that the pioneers did not have apple trees. He wished they could see the beautiful pink apple blossoms in the spring. He knew they would enjoy eating nice, crunchy apples in the fall. And they would love to have hot apple pie in the winter.

"I must think of a way to help the pioneers," Johnny said.

9

Johnny wanted to give every family an apple tree to take to Ohio. But the pioneers' wagons were already full of the things they needed. No one had room for a tree.

Then Johnny had a good idea. He decided to give the pioneers apple seeds to take with them. Whenever he ate an apple, he saved the seeds. Then he put them into leather pouches and gave them to the pioneers who passed by his farm.

"You must build a small fence after you
plant the seeds," Johnny told the pioneers.
"Deer like to eat the young plants. And you
must keep weeds from growing near the trees."

The pioneers were thankful for the seeds.
But they did not think they would have time to
take care of apple trees.

One day Johnny had an even better idea.

"I am going to go to Ohio," he told his mother and father. "I will plant apple orchards for the pioneers."

"But you will be all alone," his father said. "You will miss your family and your friends."

"And you can't just go off into the wilderness by yourself," Johnny's mother added. "Think of the wild animals. What if you get stuck in a snowstorm? And where will you sleep?"

"I will sleep right out under the sky," said Johnny. "The sky is the best roof anyone could ever have."

Johnny's parents were still worried, but they could see that he was determined to go. They helped Johnny pack his bag. His mother made him a warm coat and gave him her best cooking pan to use to make his meals.

18

Before he left, Johnny stopped at the cider mill in town. The mill used a lot of apples to make cider. Johnny asked for some apple seeds.

"Take as many as you want," the owner said.

Johnny took so many apple seeds that he couldn't fit everything back into his bag. He decided to wear the pan on his head.

"This will make a nice hat," he said.

It was not an easy trip. Johnny walked
hundreds of miles with his apple seeds.

Sometimes Johnny would stop and help a
farmer chop some wood or mend a fence.
The families Johnny helped often invited him
to have dinner with them. Soon Johnny had
many new friends.

Johnny liked sleeping out under the stars. And his mother need not have worried about wild animals. All the forest creatures loved Johnny. One time, during a terrible snowstorm, Johnny even snuggled up inside a log with a big bear.

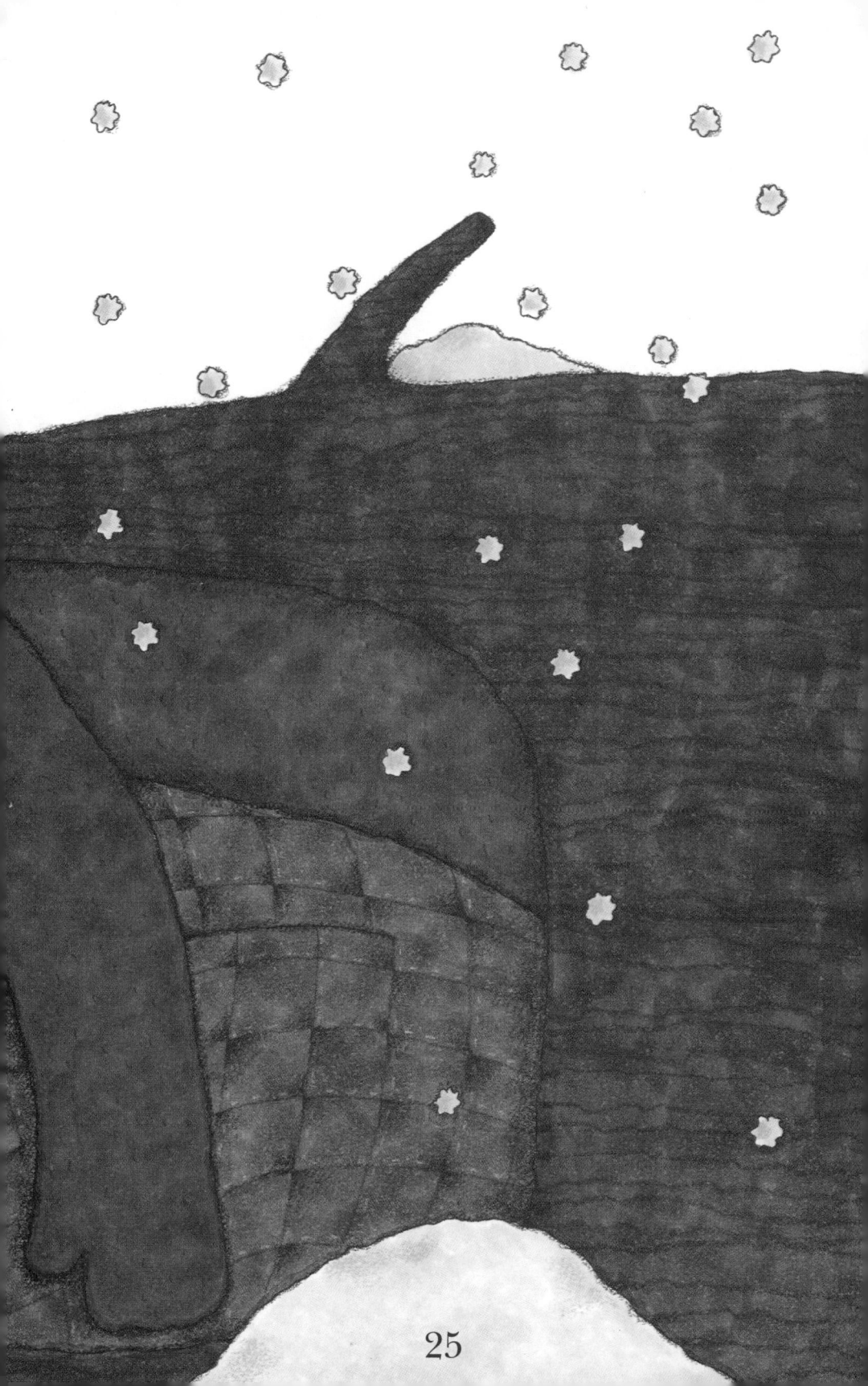

When Johnny finally arrived in Ohio, he planted seeds along the river banks. He used bushes to make prickly fences to protect the seeds.

Then Johnny moved on to another place and planted more seeds. But he always made sure to go back to care for the shoots that were already growing.

When the seedlings were big enough,
Johnny dug them up.   Then he took them to
the pioneers' homes so they could start their
own apple orchards.

"In a few years you will have apples to eat right off the tree," Johnny said. "And in the spring you will see pink apple blossoms on the trees. There isn't a prettier sight anywhere."

Johnny planted trees near hundreds of cabins in the Ohio Valley. It wasn't long before people started calling him "Johnny Appleseed."

He helped the pioneers in other ways, too. He pulled up stumps, planted corn, and built furniture for their homes.

The pioneer families looked forward to Johnny's visits.

"Wash up for supper, children," the mothers would say. "Johnny Appleseed is coming to visit us tonight!"

Johnny Appleseed spent his whole life helping people any way he could. Before he died, the Ohio Valley was blooming with apple blossoms. And some people today still think of Johnny Appleseed whenever they see apple orchards.